Clocks Are Awesome

Written and
illustrated by
Samantha Seebeck

12:12

Clocks are
awesome.

They tell you
the time.

They go tick tick tick...

...Or tick tock,
tick tock...

And there's a type of clock that goes...

CUCKOO! CUCKOO!

There are analog
clocks.

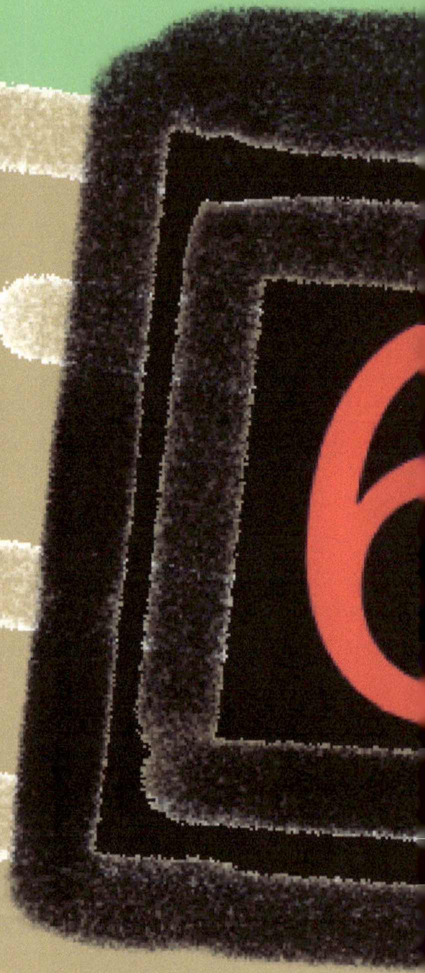

There are digital clocks.

Watches are clocks you can wear.

And alarm clocks tell you when it's time to wake up.

There's even a special clock called a grandfather clock.

The inside of a clock is filled with cogs. They are what move the hands on the outside.

There is a famous
clock called Big Ben.
It's in England.

A long time ago
people had sundials
instead of clocks.

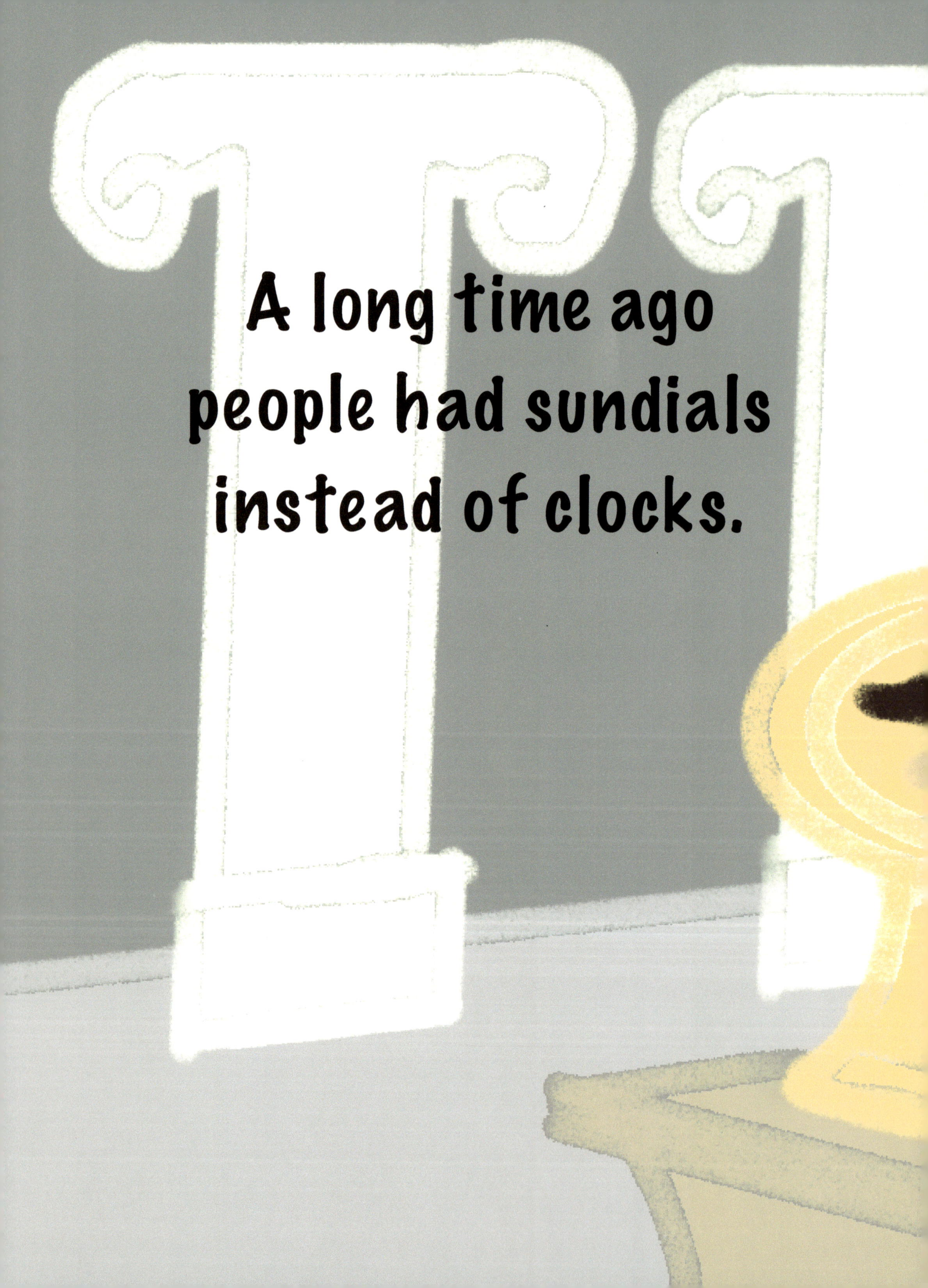

Clocks are awesome!

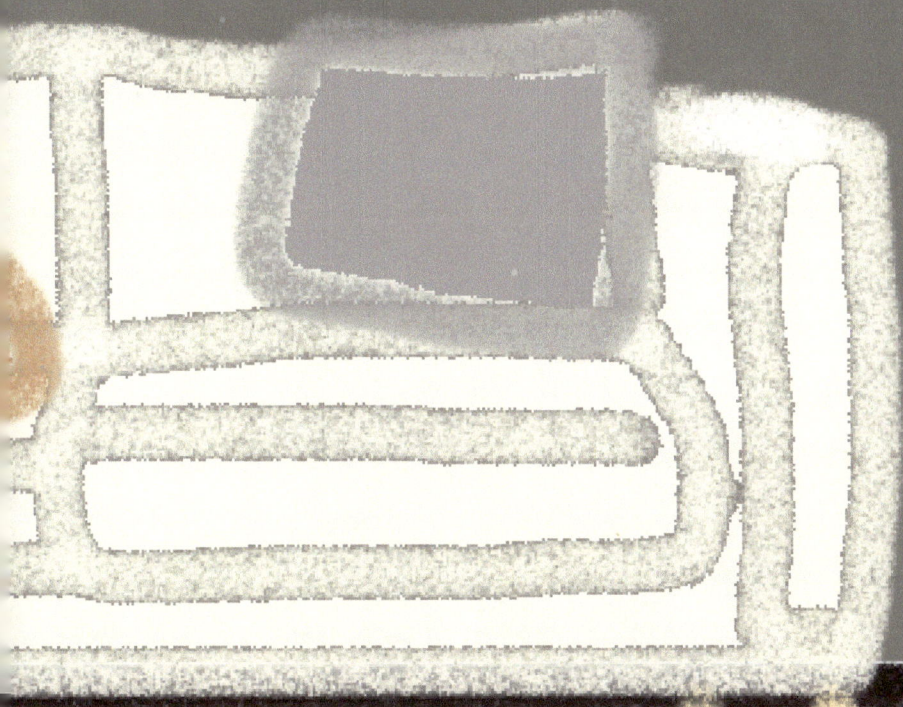

Do you think clocks
are awesome?

www.ingramcontent.com/pod-product-compliance
Lightning Source LLC
LaVergne TN
LVHW072059070426
835508LV00002B/172